ECHOES OF LIFE

AND

INDIVIDUALITY

Copyright © John Makvreng Enoch

All rights reserved. No part of this publication may be reproduced, distributed, or transmitted in any form or by any means, including photocopying, recording, or other electronic or mechanical methods, without the prior written permission of the publisher, except in the case of brief quotations embodied in critical reviews and certain other non-commercial uses permitted by copyright law.

Author- John Makvreng Enoch

ISBN-(Paperback) - 978-1-917267-58-8

ISBN (E-Book) - 978-1-917267-59-5

Year Published- 2025

Published by Nubian Republic Ltd UK on behalf of Palmwine Publishing Limited Nigeria

Email: info@palmwinepublishing.com

Address: 1A Jos Road Bukuru, Plateau State, Nigeria.

www.palmwinepublishing.com

www.raffiapress.com

www.nuciferaanalysis.com

Contents

- GENTLE DISGUISE 5
- PERSONALLY 7
- PASSIONATE MINDS 9
- PRUDENCE 11
- CONTENTED BUDDY 13
- VANITY 15
- GONE 17
- FADING INTEREST 19
- DETERMINED HEART NOT FACE 21
- BETWEEN 23
- THE OUTER SHELL 25
- CAGED FREEDOM 27
- USELESS PEERS 29
- TIME 31
- DECISIONS 33
- CHANCE 35
- TEMPERAMENT 37
- MOTHER'S LOVE 39
- COMMITMENT 41
- PROCRASTINATION 43
- DILIGENCE 45
- LEARNING 47
- BETRAYALS 49
- PRUDENT INTERACTION 50
- HUMANITY 53
- WISDOM 55
- DREAM 57
- JOURNALING 59
- TIME WAITS FOR NO ONE 61
- CHASING RIGHTLY 63
- MAKE IT RIGHT 65
- CRUSH 67
- WE THRIVE 69

HAPPINESS	71
COMMITTED WORKERS	73
PASSION	75
ERUDTIONAL INSIGHT	77
GOOD COMPANY	79
PRUDENT EXCLUSION	81
ME	83
PRUDENT LEARNING	85
LEARNING FROM OTHER'S FLAWS	87
INTENTIONS	89
REWARD	91
PASSION AND INDEPENDENCE	93
JUDGE NOT BY MERE SIGHT	95
DECISIONS	97
THOUGHTFUL GLANCE	99
RIGHT CHOICE AND TIMING	101
TRUTH	103
EITHER WAYS	105

GENTLE DISGUISE

They tell the truth sweetly

yet they walk in lies against the truth.

They do what they tell others not to do,

carrying a disguised virtue on their face.

They point at flaws with fingers,

but hide theirs in the shadows.

Reveal the deepest depth of their pretence.

PERSONALLY

He offers grand counsel to everyone.

He fails to act by his own advice, treading astray.

He speaks of truth with a completely hollow tone.

His words are like smoke, fleeting and lacking honesty.

To preach what you will not follow is pure vanity.

PASSIONATE MINDS

From alleys dim and shadows pressing.

They dreamed far beyond the wilderness of the street.

With hungry eyes, they kept reading the skies.

The ghetto's chains could not hold their sharp minds.

They had to work slow, learning patience to succeed.

Through pain and doubt, they kept sowing with faith.

From the trenches, their bright stars will rise.

PRUDENCE

Sense is her way.

She moves with a steady grace.

She calculates every step.

She listen well, and doesn't rush response.

She protects her heart, but she is still a good person.

Her mind is like a clear lantern, shining steady.

She guides those who are lost when the storm comes.

CONTENTED BUDDY

See the little food on your plate.

Many don't even find one meal.

This roof that covers us from the strong rain?

Is a big treasure

The clothes you wear and the safe bed you sleep on,

These are countless blessings.

So appreciate the little you have.

True peace is the real wealth.

VANITY

Chasing the wind, following empty trails.

When you compare yourself to another person,

Joy gets lost.

Your own path is not the same.

Stop the envy and build your own destiny.

GONE

It started with whispers and two hearts met.

But time, like a changing river, shifted the flow.

The seeds planted long ago stopped growing. .

Small wounds, left unhealed, began to spread.

Desires diverge like roads.

The flame once fierce grows dim.

Some love just fades, not from any spite.

Only fragile memory is left behind.

FADING INTEREST

When that ginger finish, everything go just dull.

The constant same thing fit make your mind weak.

When you see small failure, fear go just enter your heart.

That is how apathy will come and steal your shine.

DETERMINED HEART NOT FACE

They walk in a world very few see.

The noise from the crowd feels somehow sharp.

Their strong mind is a universe they keep inside.

They listen well, they feel things deeply, but they fear the noise.

The reason is simple: their precious energy must last.

BETWEEN

An ambivert walks in two streams.

Hugging quiet thoughts and lively dreams.

In crowds they can shine.

But they also adore solitude.

They are at ease with friends, and find peace when alone.

They get to taste the best of every side.

The greatest joy is the freedom to flow. A soul that dances to both beats.

THE OUTER SHELL

They rise with bright voices.

A simple laugh or story turns darkness into light.

The crowd is like their stage.

They draw their energy from other people's smiles.

They truly thrive in all the noise and the cheer.

CAGED FREEDOM

They call your smile a mask you wear for their own mistake.

Your light is denied.

They question your joy, and hide the grace you carry,

Monitoring you everywhere.

Your light hurts their abilities.

They wish your light will shine no more in places.

But let them think their thought because it will decay.

For your sincere heart will always outshine their fear.

USELESS PEERS

They talk for hours.

No seeds are planted, so no progress is coming.

Their plans are like smoke.

They will mock your work and laugh at the climb you are doing.

A wise person will just walk away from them fast.

Choose the builders who will make your life fruitful.

TIME

When trouble comes,

Time is telling you, "Use me well."

You need to manage your hours well,

Don't let distractions steal your way.

In these hard times, only a steady plan will bring you the victory.

DECISIONS

The choice you make shapes your future.

Every step you start becomes your story.

Opportunities arrives.

If you delay too much, that door may just close forever.

Decisions are heavy stone.

The foolish person will rush, the timid person will wait for nothing.

Choose with a clear heart, because that door may not come back.

CHANCE

A kind heart and gentle words open more doors.

Good character, builds strong bridges.

When people truly trust you, the path becomes wide.

Opportunities will surely walk right by your side.

An honourable life will always grow blessings for you.

TEMPERAMENT

The stream flow with cool temper.

Showing peace on top of the water surface.

Our moods changes.

The mountain just stand there, strong and not shaking.

The wind changes, sometimes wild, sometimes soft.

Humans have different sides

We see our real selves by how we associate.

Our own personal temperament is just mirroring everything.

MOTHER'S LOVE

In darkest chaos.

A mother's love will never end.

When you get hopeless

Her heart will always answer your call.

Overwhelming love in hard times.

Her love is eternal, her care is boundless, come what may be.

COMMITMENT

Hard work is laying the bricks always.

Each drop of sweat prepares a harvest that is secured.

Yet patience is telling you to wait and see.

Toil alone can wear out your soul, but time will complete the goal.

Both those who labour and those who wait will taste great success.

PROCRASTINATION

What you ignore now,

Gets bigger and more challenging

Living a small crack on the world, gets bigger and collapse

Taking the right steps builds.

A small leakage can turn to a river

DILIGENCE

In quiet rooms where no one is watching,

No noise and distraction.

Hidden deed becomes the root of future success.

The crowd may sleep and jest, but silent labour brings the very best.

Deeds done genuinely when alone, will surely shine when its time.

LEARNING

Learning might be frenzy

Some people think it's easy

After it gets them dizzy

Then hence they feel so lazy

BETRAYALS

Like a gentle thief with sweet smile.

Someone you helped hurt you badly.

Laughter with betrayal in its shadows.

Guide your secrets, and their lies will be exposed.

PRUDENT INTERACTION

Trust is rare.

Limit the rate of trust you give.

Guarded heart and a cautious mind can save you from pains.

Don't be deceived by words.

A watchful eye prevents the tears when people break their promises.

HUMANITY

Even in scarcity.

A true heart will still find a way to share what it has.

You don't need everything before giving.

Kindness always find a part to flow.

Give from the little you have, and remain bless.

WISDOM

Forgiveness flows like a deep water.

It covers the pain injury causes.

We give a second chance to show we are not weak people.

But don't be foolish enough to trust.

Because a broken trust is hard to fix.

So forgive to ease the anger.

Having peace of mind is one of the greatest things to have.

DREAM

Having a precise dream that burns bright.

Giving meaning to life.

Vision will always lift your tired steps forward.

A life with a dream, keeps you focus and passionate.

JOURNALING

The pages are filled with one's thoughts.

Giving insights and steps.

It's like a diary with no purpose.

Yet, it eventually gives great ideas and insights on a subject.

TIME WAITS FOR NO ONE

Anxious eyes upon the clock,

Watching time that doesn't help.

Undone work gets the dream confined,

While time unused escapes the mind.

Use every moment wisely,

For active deeds plant every seed.

CHASING RIGHTLY

Laying bricks properly and consistently.

Tired back turn the darkness to light.

Focus is sharp, ignoring fleeting distractions.

A mentor's experience and wisdom guide us.

Through mentorship, our greatness awakes.

MAKE IT RIGHT

Thousand words fill the air with empty hearts.

The tongue speaks, but deeds will prove what is true.

Promises are wind; they come and they go.

The world is moved only by the hands that work.

Let effort speak for you, for work will shine without utterances.

CRUSH

A movement that captivates

I wonder if she ever realizes the silence she fills.

I love the way she's calm and the affection in her laughter.

What I truly want is not possession, but simply her presence.

It is a quiet desire, strong enough to shape the way I breathe.

My heart definitely long for her.

WE THRIVE

In mountains of triumph and valleys of doubt.

Passion rise.

Resilience keeps us in touch.

We continue forward and never give up.

HAPPINESS

It is the warmth,

and the sound of laughter.

It is found in small victories,

in our conversations,

in the taste of food shared with someone you love.

COMMITTED WORKERS

Arriving early

Keeping things in order,

And doing the task with willingness

Attracts recognition

And deserving reward

PASSION

A fierce passion burns like fire deep in my chest.

It keeps me awake,

The discomfort is real:

Aching bones and a mind that refuses silence.

But I cannot relent,

The dream is large.

I want to thrive and prove the flame isn't meant to die.

ERUDTIONAL INSIGHT

I sit silent in school,

my voice rarely reaching the air.

People think my quietness is emptiness,

But they do not see the hours after class,

the pages I turn until my eyes ache,

the notes I write.

 I do not chase attention,

I do not perform my passion in noise.

It lives in my focus,

in the patience I give to every lesson.

When results are out,

my difference speaks for me.

Grades,

Reveal the work no one saw.

Silence is not ignorance,

it is my hidden strength.

My zeal does not need applause,

it needs only persistence.

And in the quiet,

I am building a future too loud to ignore.

GOOD COMPANY

I walk with few,

not many voices, but steady ones.

Their words are not just noise,

they are sparks that guide my steps.

In their presence I feel motivated,

their thoughts press deeper than the surface.

We share ideas that stretch the mind,

we build each other without envy.

Laughter is real,

but lessons are hidden inside it.

Mistakes become teachers,

success becomes a shared fire.

I gather strength from my friends,

We grow together.

Their impact writes itself in me,

and I carry it always.

PRUDENT EXCLUSION

I have learned to walk with opened eyes,

not only to see beauty,

but to sense the shadows moving in silence.

Trouble does not always shout,

sometimes it whispers,

sometimes it smiles with hidden teeth.

ME

Some say I am too quiet,

others think I am bold.

Some call me distant,

some imagine I am lost.

Opinions gather like dust on a table,

everyone with their own view about me.

But I have stopped trying to explain myself,

because I know who I am when silence comes.

My self-esteem is my anchor,

I remain calm when voices clash.

Value is not borrowed,

it is built within and carried forward.

PRUDENT LEARNING

I watch the world with open eyes,

not to judge, but to learn.

Every fall, every stumble I see

becomes a lesson written in silence.

When someone's trust is broken,

I remind myself to guard mine carefully.

When another wastes their hours,

I learn the weight of time

and how it cannot be reclaimed.

The failures of others are not my joy,

they are warnings carved in stone.

Their regrets whispers across my path,

urging me to walk with sense and care.

LEARNING FROM OTHER'S FLAWS

I don't need to taste every fire

to know it burns,

I only need to see the scars it leaves

and choose a wiser road.

Circumstance waits for the careless,

it traps the ones who repeat without thought.

INTENTIONS

You might have many suitors

Some might be tutors

Others might be mentors

Surely most of them are traitors

REWARD

Our basic need is food

It makes us feel so good

We have to work for it

So we can have to eat

PASSION AND INDEPENDENCE

No be who get pass dey give,

Na who wan give dey give

No too dey expect gifts from people

Just work hard and remain smart

Favor go find you

And your time go soon reach

JUDGE NOT BY MERE SIGHT

No quick judge person

No be everybody dey show-off

No judge anyhow

You fit loose-guard where your helper dey

Nobody send you

Maintain yourself and dey calm

DECISIONS

Voices that lingers in your head are your worst critics

Not every advice is used

Yet they're all important

Think well while making decisions

So you shouldn't be a victim of circumstances

THOUGHTFUL GLANCE

Not everyone that smiles with you is true

Some only plan evil against you

All cows eat grass

But not every grass is eaten by cows

Be cautious about the people you mingle with

RIGHT CHOICE AND TIMING

All work and no play

Makes Jack a doll boy

But no go use play wound wetin you suppose achieve

Work when you suppose work

And play at free time

TRUTH

Your thoughts and opinions about someone,

Doesn't change what they really are

Some let it show

Some don't show at all

So your thoughts can't change the truth

And your opinion remains your idea

EITHER WAYS

When you do good the love and hatred increases

Some people pick offense from every good you do

You get more hatred from doing bad

Regardless of how good you are

Not every loves and appreciates you

Keep on the good works

Let it last for ever

After all it's just envy

Live your life

www.ingramcontent.com/pod-product-compliance
Lightning Source LLC
Chambersburg PA
CBHW071009160426
43193CB00012B/1979